OMEGA FACTOR

John G. Henning

1st WORLD
PUBLISHING

OMEGA FACTOR

John G. Henning

© John G. Henning 2007

Published by 1stWorld Publishing
1100 North 4th St. Fairfield, Iowa 52556
tel: 641-209-5000 • fax: 641-209-3001
web: www.1stworldpublishing.com

First Edition

LCCN: 2007924925
SoftCover ISBN: 978-1-4218-9929-9
HardCover ISBN: 978-1-4218-9930-5
eBook ISBN: 978-1-4218-9931-2

TABLE OF CONTENTS

FOREWORD

This collection of verses "The Omega Factor" is about two things in general.

First, as the name omega would imply that it is an end. It is the end of a period in time for this author. There was certainly a beginning to the verses written in this collection. They are heart-felt verses, some simply reflect the time in which they occurred, some reflect just word or thought and some reflect pure fantasy. They were certainly inspired by the events of that time, the shear magnitude of love, of death, of joy, of pain, of wonder, of disappointment and of soul searching. There is no way that we can truly know what will happen in our future but we can speculate. This collection explodes with forehand knowledge unknown to the writer at that time, yet always there on the edge of the verse. There are many deep soul rooted verses in this collection, some are beyond a total focus of what they meant. Their meaning is trapped inside the writing of the words and they spill out to everyone in a different way. That is there purpose as they are not history just a part of it.

Omega as a second definition is a negatively charged particle that roams around within us and we are unaware of its existence. It is a necessity for life and the complex uncertainties of life. Negatively charged to repel off of any positive linking with anything other particle, yet a necessity to that particle. For the verses contained within this collection it is the repelling factor that would not allow a positive outcome to the heart-felt meanings, yet are the soul of the verses themselves. They are driven to draw a soul into itself and yet reject it at the same time.

Initially the thought was to create three sections, which related to specific times when the verses were written so that a reader might go through like a novel. That thought was nearly completed but it lacked a true understanding of the verses as they themselves intertwine in life at the time and are not about a set time. Then a thought to list them based upon a set time in life with no explanation but the time frame they were written. That though floated away as again the verses were not relegated to a particular time because they speak of an unknown future. They speak a truth that is sometimes hard to understand; yet they explain themselves.

Alas the choice became even though not Greek in nature but to alphabetize the verses. Therefore there is a beginning and an end. Not a true beginning as with time but a starting point which does have an end and yet they can be read in any order. The verses flow as themselves as they weave their hidden thoughts. They were written with the blood of a soul that was weeping along the path of life in a time of great love and great hurt.

So this collection places into verse the period of a man that walked through life with many weights upon him, but so many joys as well. Because the verses were written from the heart, a big heart that loved even in its hurt. That loved even through the death of life, the death of fantasy, the death of disappointment but also the love of life. For without truly loving and sacrificing there would have been no verses and no life.

ABSOLUTE SHADOW

It travels along with you no matter where you go,
It is there when there is no light.
It is a part of your being, and extension of yourself,
It does not know wrong, it does not know right.

An absolute shadow, darker than the darkest of souls,
Lost in a black hole of life, destine to live alone.
Unable to escape, attached forever to a none knowing entity,
Trapped in its own darkness, highlighted by the light,
   shamed alone.

It stretches out in the light, trying to escape, trying to get home,
It senses the loss; it knows no boundaries, yet resolves in tears.
It sheds them and they run down the blackness, no one knows,
It cannot speak, it cannot leave its shape, it lives in fear.

An absolute shadow, born from despair, felt by itself,
   alone by itself,
Forever to live wandering in the daylight.
An absolute shadow, never to be cared for, never felt for,
Forever to live wandering in the night.

AFTER THE DANCE

After the dance, will you still believe in me?
After I lead you across the floor, will you still want me?
When the music ends, will you still look at me?
When the dance is finished, will you still love me?

After the dance, will you still confide in me?
After I lead you across the floor, will you still befriend me?
When the music ends, will you still respect me?
When the dance is finished, will you still love me?

After the dance, will you still trust me?
After I lead you across the floor, will you still relate to me?
When the music ends, will you still think of me?
When the dance is finished, will you still love me?

After the dance, I will believe, want and look at you,
After I lead you across the floor, I will still confide,
  befriend and respect you,
When the music ends, I will still trust, relate and think of you,
When the dance is finished, I will still love you.

AND IF YOU

And if you believe, then I believe,
And if you fear, then I fear.
And if you love, then I love,
And if you shed a tear, then I shed a tear.

And if you listen, then I listen,
And if you dream, then I dream.
And if you feel, then I feel,
And if you scream, then I scream.

And if I believe, will you believe,
And if I fear, will you fear.
And if I love, will you love,
And if I shed a tear, will you shed a tear.

And if I listen, will you listen,
And if I dream, will you dream.
And if I feel, will you feel,
And if I scream, will you scream.

ANSWERING THE CALL

I remember the day that I first saw you,
  and I lost my heart forever,
I tried so hard not to let it go, I tried so hard, I really, really tried,
And I ached when I found out that it was only me,
That I was the only one answering the call.

This call to love or to infatuation, so much frustration
  to deal with,
It is so hard to realize that this feeling that seemed gone,
Became so alive, so real that it could not be imagination,
  no, it cannot,
Or have I gone over, am I the only one answering the call.

You are lost in the world of doubt, for you too have had love
  and lost it,
Lost it not in an instant, but over the passage of time,
  piece by piece,
Trust has become a mere word in your mindset; you do not
  seem to believe,
That there is trust in others and you can answer the call.

Only you can decide if it is wrong or if it is right, I can only
  watch and wait,
I beg that the wait will not be so long, that we lose all those
  things we could enjoy,
We can enjoy, we can be one in our time, we can feel all of
  those lost feelings,
We can really share life by answering the call.

John G. Henning

APPARITION

She came in a dream or at least it seemed that way,
I was never really sure because she mesmerized my soul.
I know that she was kind, kinder than anyone before,
Her ghostliness became so hard to understand that it
  took my soul.

But the days of bliss outlasted the days of sorrow,
For she made the sun shine when there was none.
She lifted up a heart that had been down trodden,
And she provided hope when there really was none.

I guess I felt her an apparition, because she did not stay long,
At least not in a physical sense but in a mind set.
Though her beauty was great for the eyes of the beholder,
When looking into those eyes it was as if they never met.

But of all the things that she gave to me, there was so much
  she took,
And I feel that I have grown stronger if even in my weakness.
For I know that when she was here, she gave to me her all,
And never looked over her shoulder at those with weakness.

For if she learned one thing and if I learned one thing,
It was to share the moment now, not asking why,
  not asking for forgiveness.
We were more than shadows in the night, more than
  entwined lovers,
We shared the moments rich in love and we will never need
forgiveness.

BEAUTY

How can your eyes be so beautiful?
How can they be so brown with flickers of sunshine?
How can they mesmerize and hypnotize?
How can they radiate all that love and feeling?

How can your face be so beautiful?
How can it shine with so much radiance?
How can it feel so wonderful in my hands?
How can it feel so soft when it is kissed?

How can your lips be so beautiful?
How can they speak my name so softly?
How can they be so tender with a kiss?
How can they create a smile so precious?

I don't know why all these things are so wonderful.
I don't know why I feel all these special feelings.
I don't know why you bring all this joy to me.
I guess its because all of these things are beautiful,
   all of these things are you and you are the beauty.

John G. Henning

BELIEVING IN YOU

Believing in you has changed my life,
Believing in you has shown me that I can still love,
Believing in you has opened a closed door,
Believing in you has allowed me to love.

Believing in you has lifted my soul,
Believing in you has placed my feeling on the line,
Believing in you has created an undying trust,
Believing in you has pushed me to the line.

Believing in you has mirrored feelings in my heart,
Believing in you has fulfilled a fantasy into a dream,
Believing in you has forced the emotion to the top,
Believing in you has caused reality to enter the dream.

Believing in you is all that I can do,
Believing in you is all that I want to do,
Believing in you is all that I need to do,
Believing in you is loving you.

BIG HEART

There have been times in my life that I thought I had a big heart,
Especially when it was broken and the hurt cut deep.
I remember true love, that love that hurts so badly yet it is the
  only true one,
True at that moment, true as long as everyone believes it is
  ours to keep.

There are times when this heart has been big, it has loved many,
Some loved in whole, some loved in parts, some loved inside.
When you think that there cannot be any other,
  real becomes alive again,
All of the pain, all of the joy returns, all those things grow inside.

When you feel love, when you know that it is real again,
Sometimes there is no real solution, life has created more hurt,
  more fear.
We have learned in those times when love was denied or just
  placed away from us,
We learn that we have to take the chance; there can be
  no more fear.

I can never promise that life will not provide unknown avenues,
I can never guarantee that life will not cause other lives to part.
I can only give you all the love that I feel, all the kindness
  you deserve,
All the warmth and comfort in your life, all that is yours, your
  life, all of my big heart.

John G. Henning

CANDLE

With a burst of energy illuminating in bright colors,
So bright that it is blinding, the spark is a light.

As the glare dies down, the flame becomes all enveloping,
It rushes through the core and embraces the new wick.

The flame is a burning amber, destined to provide life,
And it burns so very slowly bonded to the wax stout.

At times a rush of air will try to end the flame,
But it survives in its youth, stronger so it will prevail.

The slow burn and forces outside may stifle the flame's advance,
An abyss may form and the flame is not as bright.

The flame gets smaller and smaller with time,
  but never gives up,
And as with life reaches the point grown thick.

Through all of the times and all of the tribulations,
One day the candle is blown out.

So now the wick is burned away and the candle serves
  no purpose,
Not like life, but so mirrored, life tries and does prevail.

CHANGE

I woke up this morning, even that flesh turned fat was tight,
I have been so wound up lately, so tight, if touched I would
  break apart,
There has just been so much change.

I remember when everything seemed so easy,
  there were no worries,
Love flowed like a river taking me beyond barriers
  I never knew existed,
All of it such a great change.

Then the birthing came, a new experience, caught up in
  grand emotion,
I will always remember the growth, the care, the new life,
What a wonderful change.

Then life seemed to stop, as if there was a slow motion camera,
Each frame a different part and not really coming together
  in a story,
This story, which is caught up in change.

Alas a new turn has come along, it feels so good, it feels so right,
Maybe it is not new, just a new way of thinking,
  too much thinking,
I don't know if I can accept this change,
I don't know if I want to change.

John G. Henning

COMMUNICATION

I sometimes keep to myself all those things that I should
  say to you,
Not only the loving things but also the feelings that I
  have inside.
I keep to myself those thoughts; I should share with you,
They belong to you as well as me, they do not belong inside.

I try very hard to remember this communication,
But I sometimes get lost in the thought process, not saying
  how I feel.
You must sometimes think that I do not want to tell you
  those things,
That is not true, I want you to know how I feel.

I try not to hold those emotions inside, because they are so real,
I do not want you to think that I don't care about you.
I do with all of my heart in spite of all my fears,
Because those emotions belong not just to me, but also to you.

So if sometimes I seem distant, question me, I am waiting
  for you,
I am trying to put all of my emotional trust in you, to commu
  nicate those feelings.
I have at times not been able to do that, but I am trying
  very hard,
I am trying hard to overcome my fears, trying to prove
  my feelings.

I know that with each breath that I take, I am so close to you,
There is nothing more I would want then to share with you
  my heart.
But part of that sharing is a sharing of all those fears we all face,
I will try harder, will you help, can you believe in this heart.

When I need to talk, will you listen to me?
When you need to talk, I will listen to you.
Together we can learn to communicate all those fears,
Together we can learn about me and you.

John G. Henning

CROSSOVER

As much as we may think that we are in control,
We never really are in control other than at the moment.
If we go with the moment, sometimes we can last forever,
If we do not go with the moment, we lose the chance for
  the event.

There is always a time when we have to crossover into
  that unknown,
We venture into that area where we matter more than others.
We are not selfish, we are aware of all of the feelings,
  their feelings,
We are who we must be; we cannot be like the others.

If the feeling is so deep that there is no other world,
Then how can we just walk away and deny all those feelings.
Walking away denies us the only time in our lives,
When this event is real beyond anything in the world, beyond
  others feelings.

There is truth in real love; there is truth in believing,
It is beyond that dream, when the dream is real and you
  must crossover.
Please do not deny your own existence, those who love you
  will always love you,
Believe in your own heart, not just the logic, I am real, I am
  true, crossover.

EMBRACING LOVE

There have been so many joyous times when I embraced love,
When it was in these hands, when they held someone so
  very close.
But now they hold something that is empty,
Empty only because of fear of the yesterdays.

I can only try to show all that love has not left,
It is here as long as you believe in it, in the real feelings.
The trust you must now believe in is hard because
  of memories,
There has to be more happy days, then sad days.

So I am here, I am waiting in my love, waiting for you,
Leave all of those memories behind, so we can travel
  on to love.
You have been there before; you have felt it grow new,
Let us open up our hearts, let us start and keep embracing love.

John G. Henning

EMOTIONAL POLICE

They are everywhere, next to you, next to me, in you and in me.
When will it all end, or will it never end.
They play with our emotions; casting them away, bring them
  back, hurting us,
Can we be saved and to what end?

The emotional police stiff in their decisions, no freedom here.
And when they break it all apart are they happy?
Never, because the emotion they wanted is already gone, they
  have destroyed it.
And they or you or us or we or whoever is never happy.

EMOTIONAL RESCUE

Sometimes we cannot see that which is near,
And sometimes we cannot feel that which is dear.
But we always know when there is wrong or we don't
   understand,
Why those we loved no longer care and by our standards
   can disappear.

Sometimes we forget that we once could really feel,
But now that love has gone astray, broken the love seal.
A pact made the day love walked in etched golden sand,
Washed away by the tide of uncaring, leaving hurt that is so real.

We do get other chances to try to make it work, one more time,
And sometimes we turn away, away from a new love for the
   sake of time.
Because it becomes our enemy like desolate and barren land,
We cannot let that new love go, because there is never
   enough time.

When given the chance at emotional rescue, we cannot
   walk away,
For on that day we turn away, we turn away forever from
   that day.
There cannot be a waiting period, for that love is real and true,
If we leave it today, we leave it forever and can never regain
   that day.

John G. Henning

So if you are there trapped in a void, lost in dilemma,
  unable to chose,
For you feel that the choice would be wrong and you
  would lose.
There are no other days, if love falls through your
  clenched hand,
For you will always know that it was there, there for
  you to use.

So don't think so hard, don't think so deep that love passes by,
For everyone will know the truth with your every sigh.
Because hurt cannot hide behind a smile, it turns the
  smile bland,
And the love that was thought to be true, has turned into a lie.

So when that emotional rescue pounds on your front door,
Do not turn it away, do not slap its face, do not throw it
  on the floor.
You have earned that right to be happy and to live your
  life true,
It will walk with you, it will live for you, it will last
  forever more.

EMPTY DAY

I awoke this morning; the room was as dark as the night
outside.
My mind racing along knowing that today was a day that
would be empty.
For today you would not be within my sight and I would not
hear your voice.
And this day would be void and empty.

It is not as bad as an empty day where a loved one has
passed on.
And their voice and smells and visions of their faces bring tears.
All of those tears are not sorrow, for some reflect all of the joy.
That was a part of that loved one and we no longer have
any fears.

It is not as bad as an empty day where the one we love does
not exist.
Not in mind, not in body, not in front of us, transparent to all
of our feelings.
All those tears of sorrow, for they never ever reflect any joy.
For long ago the part that may have loved us, left us without
any feelings.

John G. Henning

Although my day may be empty today, I hope that it will be
   filled tomorrow.
For the emptiness is not from death, but only for this one
   given day.
And I hope never to stand in front of you and not know whom
you are.
For I will always feel the way I do, and never give you an
   empty day.

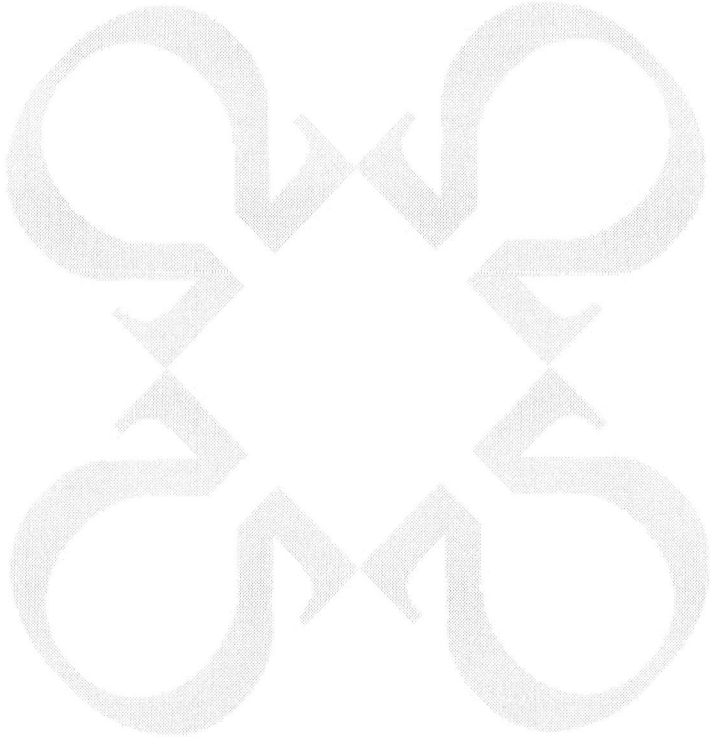

EVERYDAY

Everyday I can picture your smiling face, when you are not
  in sight,
Everyday I can hear your beautiful voice, when your voice
  cannot be heard,
Everyday I can feel your gentle touch, when your touch cannot
  be felt,
For even when you are not here, I am in love with you
  everyday.

FIRST DAY OF FALL

I awoke before dawn's light to experience the first day of fall,
As I stepped out from the doorway, the crisp air creating a
blanket around me.
I breathed in the chilled air glad that I had warmed my insides
with breakfast,
Knowing that I might not return soon, carrying just a pad and
pen and an apple with me.

I walked down the path I had walked so many times before,
this my secret place,
Watching the sun twinkle reflections of light toward my naked
eye, squinting in the glare.
My feet change sounds from the crunch of dirt to the
resounding sound of wood,
The gate increasing in anticipation of this relationship
transformed into an affair.

The seat is damp from dew, quickly wiped away by hand and
spread out on dry cloth,
To rest the body on this bench faded by weather and wear, to
rest both heart and soul.
Rays of radiant heat kissing flesh numbed by the chill, melting
away all cares,
I love the feel, I love the smells, I love the sights, I love bearing
my soul.

Today is a day of writing to you, you know who you are, the
  nemesis already created,
The need is deep to clear the air like it is clear in front of me in
  my existence.
I remember the day we met, the day I loved, the way I felt pain,
  the day I almost died,
For so long I have fought the need, the desire to reveal, today
  there is no resistance.

I hadn't thought that so much would become of something so
  small and so one sided,
It was always wrong, never right, never right in my head, but
  always right in my soul, in my heart.
But it was always right in the way I felt, the way that I feel and
  the way I will always feel,
Life and family has placed an impenetrable barrier, to chastise a
  family is not in my heart.

So today on this first day of fall, I sit hoping to tell all with this
  pen and pad,
The little touches, the little kisses, the small times together
  without any care.
Were they the same for you, did you feel these same feelings, I
  think not,
I have stayed away so long, so not to touch and not to kiss and
  not to dare.

Not dare to break the promise in my heart, the one that keeps
  me away from the love,
The promise burned inside my heart from years gone by and
  memories faded.
As much as there is peace and joy here, there has been so
  much conflict,
I fear that if it goes on longer, even that which is the essence of
  my soul shall be faded.

John G. Henning

So today I claim my right to love, to care, to feel, to touch, to
  hold, to kiss, to be the boy again,
Be aware that I am coming and that I bring more love than you
  have felt in years.
For I know all of the sadness you have felt and all of the
  loneliness, and maybe even pain,
I can no longer wait; I can no longer stand on the side and
  watch smiles with tears.

The sun has risen high in the sky and the insides crave some
  thing to eat, and thirst,
Open up the jacket to take the apple from within, kept warm
  by cloth and body heat.
The crunch of the apple awakes the realization that all sounds
  had been deaden,
While the concentration of thought has been alive, no feeling
  of sounds and heat.

It has grow warmer as the heat reflects off the water, but the
  water will not be warm,
Walking to the edge of the dock and bending down cupping
  clear cool water to drink.
Drinking deeply unaware of the traces of water traveling along
  aged skin cracks,
Dripping water back onto a reflection, looking lost in despair,
  lost unable to think.

But I do think, think of all the times when the smiles were
  always there ready to enjoy,
Not buried in the mire of disillusionment, trapped in an
  imaginary room, a reality tomb.
Let us awaken those feelings; let us live the life that is before
  us, not one that is behind,
The apple is finished it has the hue of brown, toss it into the
  water, to a watery tomb.

I must remove the jacket and sit on the bench; my mind is
   ablaze with story,
Remember when we went to the park; remember the walks, the
   jokes, the joy.
Or was that just me and never you, did I imagine all
   those things,
Has my mind gone far beyond even those things remembered
   by the boy?

I remember your children's illnesses and joys and your mate's
   changes in life,
You never tried to change and kept the smile pasted on like a
   clown's face.
I saw inside the eyes that cried when no one was around to
   kiss the tears away,
I saw the change so subtle as it was, each day a little more,
   until there was no real face.

The shell has been there too long; please look as I do in the
   reflection of the water,
Where has the girl gone, has reality taken all that there was and
   buried it deep.
So deep that even when true love faces you, the fear of change
   places heavier guilt,
That you cannot think straight, all avenues look like dead
   ends, and there is no sleep.

There was a time when laughter was abound and your life was
   so happy,
Maybe you can make the change; maybe you can get it back,
   maybe if you try harder.
I know that I cannot help you since I am too close to you, but
   do not shut me out,
With all of my heart and soul and all my desire, I can but try
   even harder.

John G. Henning

The sun sets and the moon rises, it has been such a long day,
  reflective thought has taken the day away,
The pad seems to have no more paper left and the ink is
  streaked and etched like lace.
The night has cooled and I put on the jacket trying the keep
  away the chills already there,
I turn to walk the path I have walked a hundred times headed
  for the fireplace.

As I reach the door I turn to face the moon so full and bright,
  your real face is there,
If you can look into that moon and see my face, know that we
  will not fall.
Then there is hope, how small it is, that we may love for who
  we are,
This letter will make great kindling for this the first day of fall.

FANTASY

Be not afraid of those things that abound on the outside,
For they are not the real fear, they are merely a focus,
Look towards that which is inside hidden wrapped in torment,
For there is nothing to be afraid of, nothing to fear and nothing
  to bring torment,
For it is all but fantasy.

Be not so smug to not see or feel others close within grasp,
For they are real, they do exist, they are your life,
Look towards the light that brings the hope and dreams,
For there is nothing to smug about, nothing that is not real and
  nothing that is beyond the light,
For it is not true fantasy.

Be not the one to turn me away for I am that which is true,
For you know and in knowing believe even as you don't,
Look towards the reality with half an open eye,
For there is nothing to turn away from, nothing more to know
  and nothing to do with reality,
For I am fantasy.

John G. Henning

FEELING TOMORROW

It can be so real that feeling of happiness, when there is so
   much to give,
It is so wonderful to understand all those thoughts, to feel
   every day.
Feeling tomorrow, knowing that there is a tomorrow,
Never ever giving thought that there would not be another day.

There is so much that plays with the heart as it travels
   its course,
Trying to believe that there is this real feeling, this real need.
A need for tomorrow, hoping that there can be a tomorrow,
Forever thinking about how wonderful this special need.

Passage of feelings from heart and soul, allowed to set in
   the mind,
Believing in the thought that there is a great wonderful belief.
A belief in tomorrow, wanting to be there tomorrow,
Finding out that there is more than just a belief.

There is so much for us to be thankful for, to believe in,
All the feelings that reside in the thoughts of tomorrow.
We know how we feel today, we know want we want,
We want to be real; we want to be feeling tomorrow.

FOGGY LOOKING GLASS

Who is that there? Is it I?
Am I that person glaring back in rage?

Where has the smile gone? Has it disappeared?
Did someone walk away with it?

Has someone stolen that happiness?
Have they trampled joy into the ground?

Where are they? Who are they?
Do they belong here?

What have they done with me?
Why have they caused this frown?

Why can I not see that smile?
Why can I not see?

It's just a foggy looking glass.

John G. Henning

FROZEN LOVE

There is the first time when love comes into your heart,
It fills it up with joy, joy that seems to be forever.
Yet it resides for a little while, never really staying long,
And yet it will reside forever.

We try at this time to freeze that love,
We try to make it stay, not wanting it to leave us.
We are trapped by the thought that it will leave us,
And we will never have that love.

As life goes on, we feel love again, or still feel its first kiss,
Our hearts fill again so much that it will burst, if we cannot
   have these feelings.
Yet it is those same feelings, which can bring on the pain,
The other side, the dark side of those wonderful feelings.

We try again to freeze this love,
We do not want to think of the pain within us.
We want to remember only the joy that was in us,
And we will never leave that love.

Somehow, some way, we have found that feeling of love,
Even after it was crushed, or when it was bruised with pain.
We are lost in our hearts conviction, embodied in our souls,
No matter all of the teachings, we still can feel the pain.

We now freeze this love,
We close the door so it will not leave.
We do not realize that we will make it leave,
And we find we cannot freeze love.

John G. Henning

HALF PAST

The piercing shrill wakes the numbed brain drunk because of
lack of sleep,
A shooting numbed hand slams the clock begging on and on,
awake, awake to me.
The sound dies like the phantom conversation pause, created
in an unknown instance,
The semi-focused eye glancing towards the red reveler, it's half
past three.

There is no return to the depths of unconsciousness, it is not
allowed, it is forbidden,
Electrical impulses flashing across the mind, why do I exist,
am I alive.
The meadow is green and the flowers many, with smells so
sweet, and sight so great,
Snapping open as quickly as a blink, the sight sees the red
essence beaming half past five.

It has taken so long to dredge to this place, this holder of
broken dreams and schemes,
Prodded by stares, gestured in elegance, voiced locations of
places other than heaven.
Is there no end to this grinding repetition of meaningless
matter, pounded into obscurity?
It has been forever, at least there is this fear of forever, only
half past seven.

Many vows have been broken, made to voiceless entities, words
lost in infinity,
Faster than light itself, careening towards the end, headed
aimlessly to the end of life.
Where did the hours, days, years go, they have never left, they
have been used to their limit,
There will always be time, time to reflect, time to accomplish,
it is only half past life.

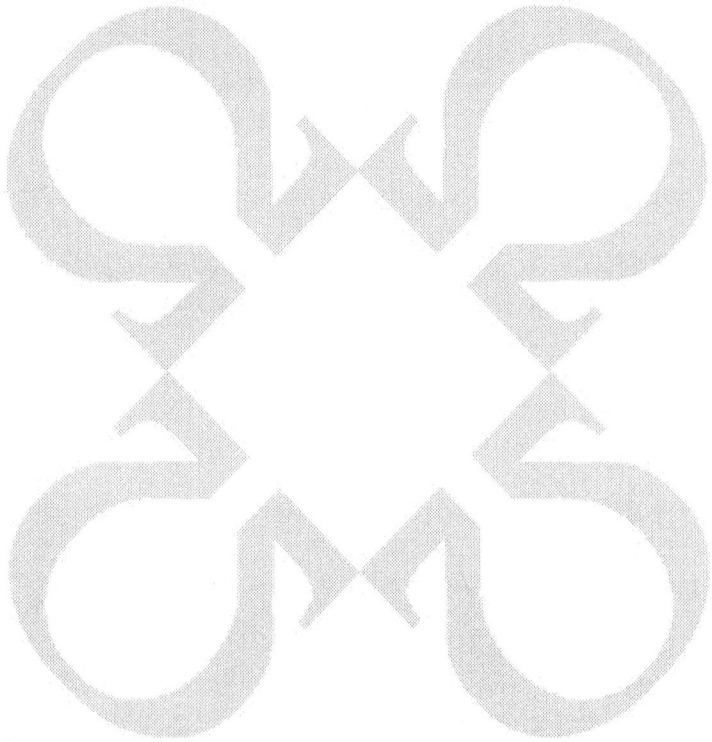

John G. Henning

HANDSHAKE

Who's to say when things happen, when emotions are triggered?
When feelings become alive, when realization of calm
  approaches,
Was it a look, was it a smile, was it a handshake?

I remember when the dark clouds opened up and the sun came
  shining through,
It was the first time I touched you, it was a handshake,
Oh, we had hugged the friend hug, we had gazed at each other,
  we had new thoughts,
But it wasn't until that handshake, that first true touch did
  life beckon.

I had never realized in my life what joy there could be in
  the world,
I had never realized all of those things taken for granted,
Passing me by like picketed fences viewed from a moving car,
Past before they were seen or enjoyed, if even for a second.

All of that changed as feelings grew stronger and hugs longer,
We both felt the change, so afraid of these changing emotions,
How could we feel this way? Did we ever feel this way before?
Why did the feelings come now? Why in this time of life?

The first gentle kiss, the warm embrace, the touch of hand
  on face,
Bursting open, all those things thought lost, though buried
  forever,

Exploring each other's heart and soul and mind, looking
  for answers,
Are there any? Do they exist? What is this new life?

Even today with all those things having become memories,
  revisited everyday,
With all the warmth and tenderness, shared for a second or a
  minute or an hour,
Even today the feelings are there in that handshake.

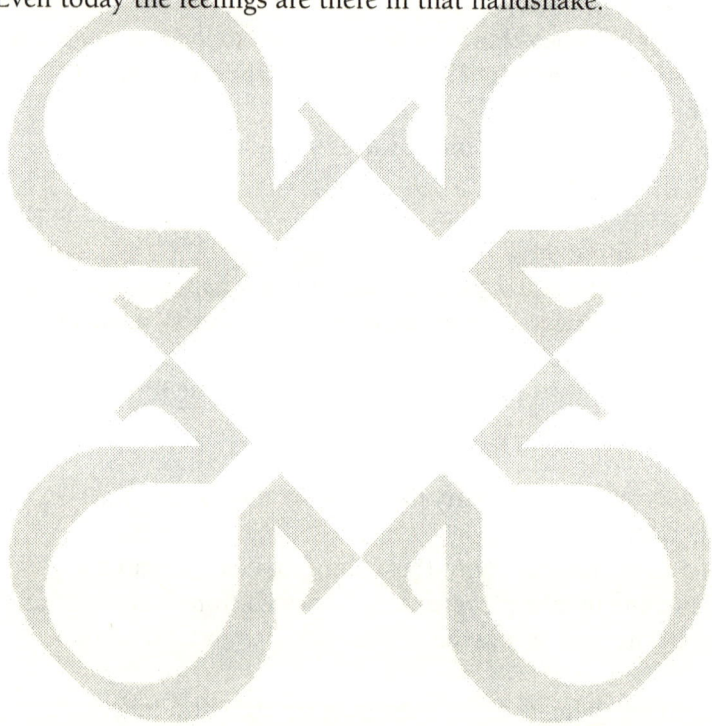

HAPPINESS IS A WARM SMILE

Sometimes everyone else knows, but we don't,
Sometimes we are so into each other that others are far in
  the dark.
In a room full of people do we not find each other?
Do we not feel each other when we are so far apart?

Everything else that we know, we are so aware of, it is our life,
But we become confused and our minds wander into this
  strange land.
Not strange at one time in life, but so overburdening now,
It seems not to be able to be satisfied, where do we start?

Neither of us knows which way to go, is there a path to save us,
We want to do what is right, even if not right for us.
So we will ache and agonize and leave each other's life for no
  reason,
They will never know that happiness is a warm smile.
They will never know that they washed it away forever.

HAPPY HEART

I feel the rush of my heart as I look into your eyes,
I cannot believe that you are the one that I love.
But my heart knows, this happy heart,
And it thanks you everyday for this love.

Each beat is a beat that knows your name,
That pushes out warmth that calls for your touch.
Feeling it everywhere, in the depths of my mind,
I cannot leave this place; I cannot leave your touch.

When I sigh I feel the world looks at me,
Yet they cannot know the way this heart feels.
That it is so happy, words are not enough,
That no one but I really knows how it feels.

I want to share this happy heart with you,
For you have been the saving grace in my life.
I have it waiting for you, every beat for you,
Awaiting the touch of your happy heart in my life.

John G. Henning

HAVE I BEEN, HAVE YOU BEEN

Have I been so blind that I could not see the fear?
Have you been so blind that you could not see me near?
Have I been so blind that I could not cry the tear?
Have you been so blind that you could not see me dear?

Have I been so cold as not to understand how you feel?
Have you been so cold as not to understand how I deal?
Have I been so cold as not to understand how you heal?
Have you been so cold as not to understand how I kneel?

Have I been so into myself that I have lost the end of my rope?
Have you been so into yourself that you have lost the will
    to cope?
Have I been so into myself that I just sit and mope?
Have you been so into yourself that you have lost all hope?

Have I been so much without love that I cannot feel your love?
Have you been so much without love that you cannot feel my
    love?
Have I been so much without love that I cannot have your love?
Have you been so much without love that you cannot have my
    love?

HUGS

What is this great force, that binds us together.
When we hold each other close and the world melts away.

We can feel each other's bodies and great embracing arms.
We can feel our hearts beating within each other's breast.
We can feel the tender cheek and wisp of hair.
We can feel our chest rise as it swells up in joy.
We can smell the sweet fragrance of love.

And we dare not let go because we might lose that feeling
    forever.
We squeeze tighter and tighter, becoming one.
And when we do separate the feeling never leaves.
It has become a part of us a part of our life, it cannot be taken
    away.

What is this great force, that binds us together.
When we hold each other close and the world melts away.
It is more than embrace more than arms locked in sweet
    happiness; it is hugs.

John G. Henning

I AM YOU

With the tiniest of touch, you warm my heart,
That touch that melts away all the fears,
That touch that tells me I am you.

With the warmest smile, you steal my soul,
That smile that turns away the reality,
That smile that tells me I am you.

With the slightest of glances, you pierce my mind,
That glance that turns the world away
That glance that tells me I am you.

With the sweetest voice, you fill my ears,
That voice that drowns out all that past sorrow,
That voice that tells me I am you.

With the purist of heart, you steal my life,
That heart that makes my life worthwhile,
That heart that tells me I am you.

I am you, I have know for so long,
I have tasted your sweet feelings; I have held your precious
   trust,
I have heard your name echoing in my soul,
I am you, are you me?

I DON'T UNDERSTAND

I don't understand why the sky is blue sometimes,
And then it is so dark I cannot see.
I don't understand how life brings such joy,
And then it takes it all away.
I don't understand it at all.

I don't understand why the wind blows over the land,
And then becomes so still it does not exist.
I don't understand how the heart brings such feelings,
And then clouds them in uncertainty.
I don't understand it at all.

I don't understand why the sun shines with great warmth,
And then cannot turn away the cold.
I don't understand how the soul felt such wonders,
And then lost its way.
I don't understand it at all.

I don't understand why rain can help in its own way,
And then turn itself against that which it helps.
I don't understand how love can be so wonderful and real,
And then hide away.
I don't understand it at all.

John G. Henning

IF I COULD

If I could I would take your heart to the same place
  mine resides,
In that place where hearts are free and there are no boundaries,
  no stopping love.
Hearts swell with anticipation of the knowledge of love
  returned,
If I could I would take your heart where my heart is in love.

If I could I would take your soul higher than it has ever
  been before,
Higher than anyone has ever taken it, higher than life itself,
  higher then we can hope,
Souls intertwined in the love of life, love of others, love of self,
If I could I would take your soul where my soul is filled with
  hope.

If I could I would take your mind along the path of feelings,
Knowing that there is so much good there, some much for us
  to live.
Minds coming together in realization of all of those things we
  cannot deny,
If I could I would take your mind where my mind wants to live.

For if I could, our hearts would reside together,
For if I could, our souls would soar forever,
For if I could, our minds would bind together,
For if I could, love would be here forever.

I GUESS

I guess I came here because I wanted you,
I guess I have always wanted you, to be near you, to hold you.
There have been times when I just couldn't because I thought
   that you did not want me,
Even now I sometimes find it hard to believe that you do,
It is something that I always wanted, wanting you.

I guess I came here because I needed you,
I guess I have needed you from the first day I saw you.
You lit up a life that had grown dark and had a very deep need,
A need you fill at times and at times you just turn it away,
Understanding your need has been the biggest challenge and I
   take it on in full stride,
That was something missing in my life, needing someone,
   needing you.

I guess I came here because I love you,
From the first time our eyes met, I guess I have always loved
   you.
For me it was instant, taking my heart away, encircling my
   soul, numbing my mind,
For you it has been a long trail, shadowed with doubt and
   uncertainty, lost in thought,
Knowing that a choice decided, a commitment made, would
   maybe cause pain and loss,
I came here because I love you; love me as I love you.

John G. Henning

I.L.Y.A.L.

It has sometimes been a rocky road,
Not knowing when or why the emotions changed.
Only knowing that those emotions could not be hidden,
Knowing that I like you a lot.

Sometimes it seems so wrong, but at times it seems so right,
How can this emotion roller coaster my heart.
When I feel this good inside, when my heart sings,
Because I like you a lot.

There is some fear here, some fear of the unknown,
It is real, as real as life itself and it must be dealt with,
Never wanting this emotion to stop; yet searching for an
  answer,
For I like you a lot.

When the road is no longer rocky, when my emotions are in
  full view,
When I know that it is only right, and my heart breaks out in
  song for all.
When there is not more fear of the unknown, and the answer
  echoes in my heart,
Then will I love you a lot.

INNOCENT CHILD

I remember when I was so very young, when all there was,
  was life,
And all of the people, all of the relatives, the aunts, the cousins,
  the grandmothers.
Were young and played with me and held me close.

But there were days that turned to black when there was no
  life,
And the grandfather, the uncle, the great relative went away,
And I no longer saw them for I lost them.

And as I have grown and learned to live with death as part
  of life,
I look at my young and innocent child and know they will
  learn the pain,
With eyes swelled up together, joined by this dark moment
  in time,
I remember when I was so very young, when all there was,
  was life.

John G. Henning

INTERSTATE

The day is clear with small clouds floating across a blue sky,
It is beautiful day, it is wonderful.
I am so full of love today, more than yesterday, more than
   tomorrow,
My feelings are so deep that no words can express what I say.

I travel along this interstate with many others lost in their
   own thoughts,
What are those thoughts, who knows, we live in our
   own mind.
I know how I see this day; I know how I feel this day,
What a special day for me, you are so alive in my mind.

I see your face in the clouds, that lovely smiling face,
It is my beacon in the day, it illuminates my heart.
With the window open, sounds in my ears and a rush of air
   past my face,
I hear your voice in the wind echoing in my heart.

I feel the breeze play against my face like tiny fingers,
They are the touches that you give to me, they are your
   feelings.
The air smells sweet above all of the stale air,
Because in my soul the only air that exists is generated by
   your feelings.

I travel along this interstate towards you, towards that which
  is you,
For the miles do not matter when there is so much love.
Time passes quickly; I will be in your arms soon,
Because forever you will be in my heart, my sweet love.

JOHN'S PASS

It could have been any day, any place in the world,
But it happened when you turned away from reality for that
    instant,
All of the fears disappeared, if only for that instant,
But then you let reality walk back into your life.

We can run, we know how to run, we fear the run,
But you've wanted to run for so long, yet could not run
    far enough,
That blank bare wall unyielding when in a reality check,
Has turned away all of those flights which were so easy to do
    in life.

John's Pass is just a faint glimmer lost in a blazing inferno
    of guilt,
You didn't run far enough, you didn't try hard enough, you lost
    the moment,
We take our chances in the safe world, or in an obscure fake
    cloak of fantasy,
Life is more than a moment and a moment can be more
    than life.

JUST FOR ONE MOMENT

Just for one moment, I would like the world to stop,
Just for one moment, I would like to be with you.
Just for one moment, I would want to love you,
Just for one moment, I would want you to love me.

Just for one moment, I would like to be in your heart,
Just for one moment, I would like those we love to know,
Just for one moment, I would want the world to know,
Just for one moment, I would want you to know all that is me.

I would give up all my riches for just one moment,
I would give up all that I have for just one moment,
I would give up my heart and soul for just one moment
  with you.

John G. Henning

KISS ME, MISS ME

When I hurt from pain or sorrow, kiss me,
When I leave your side for an hour, miss me.
When I am happy and joyous, kiss me,
When I visit someone ill, miss me.
When we are in love's embrace, kiss me,
When I am not in your arms, miss me.
When I stray too far, kiss me,
When I am so close to your heart, miss me.
When I have gone because you did not kiss me,
When everything is over, will you miss me?

KNOWING ABOUT YESTERDAY

We pass through life, just once,
We find those things that make us happy, maybe once,
Yet sometimes we get that second chance, knowing about
   yesterday.

Life is such a wonder; we sometimes let it pass by,
Not because we want it to, not because we don't try,
We try to remember those days past, knowing about yesterday.

We share many things with others, our lives, our loves,
We understand each other for those times we are together,
We are alive; we are so real, knowing about yesterday.

Knowing about yesterday makes us strong, strong only in fact,
We learn, but we cannot use just yesterday's dreams.
Today is the start of so many new things, it is our life,
Knowing about yesterday, is knowing about our dreams.

John G. Henning

LADY, MISS LADY

They did not mean any disrespect, when they called you lady,
Because if they knew you like I do, they would only have
  respect,
They may have meant the word respectfully as I, but that
  wasn't what you heard,
For they did not know nor could have know that you were
  my lady.

You have been so many things to me, the girl, the woman,
  the love,
But most of all you have been that person, who walks in
  elegance,
And holds herself so tall and straight and never lets the world
  change her,
For I have and always will respect you as my lady.

I have felt your sensitive touch and kissed your lips and held
  you so close,
I have smelled your sweet hair and nestled in the nape
  where it lies,
Forever to remember to smells, the sights and the sounds that
  have surrounded us,
Never from my memory will they escape, because they are
  my lady.

So even though they may use that word, you seem to find to
  be harsh,
But it is the same word that I use for you and you know I love
  you so,
They may think they see the woman older than themselves,
But they will never know the miss inside, my lady, miss lady.

John G. Henning

LINE IN THE SAND

Imaginary or real this line in the sand, created out of
 protection,
Protection for all those that we love, but not ourselves.
Maybe for ourselves, for that safe feeling, no commitment,
 no hurt,
Can you be that way forever?

This line in the sand subject to the littlest of wind,
 blown apart,
So much time spent in wondering if they will be aware,
Aware of what? When they are not aware of what they do not
 give now,
Can I be that way forever?

We have both asked to cross over that line in the sand,
In our thoughts and our feelings regardless of turning away,
Shall I cross over or shall you? Can we wait another second?
Can we be this way forever?

LOVE LAKE

In the course of time there always seems to be that time,
That time being when love blossoms.
It doesn't really matter when it happens, in our youth,
  the middle years, the golden years,
The thing that matters is that it happens that it is real.

In my youth was the time that love came to me and at the time
  I didn't know that it existed,
We never forget the time and the place, and neither shall I.
It was at an uncle's lake, a real lake owned by him, at least I
  thought so then,
I loved the water, the smells, the air, and I never knew how I
  could really feel.

A name is but a name, except when you fall in love,
So like some grant stone, her name is etched in my mind.
I would learn that she had come to stay with an aunt having
  lost her parents.
She felt she should have been with them; she had a very
  heavy heart.

As I walked towards the end of the dock, to sit in my spot,
I noticed it taken by some stranger.
They couldn't have know it was my spot, I would explain,
I hoped that this new friendship would not have an awful start.

John G. Henning

She sat there with swollen eyes; I didn't know what to say,
So I offered to leave her in her solitude.
She beckoned me to sit and I sat for what must have been
   an eternity
I did not look at her, her low sobs tugging at my heart; I gazed
   around the lake.

A path, no, more a trail hugged the lake its full length,
I had placed my foot on every exposed surface.
As I followed that path with my eyes, I thought that soon I
   would be walking there,
My eyes coming full circle, returned before me gazing into
   the lake.

She did not talk to me, but I somehow knew she wanted to,
Instead she touched my hand, I flinched.
I gazed at her hazel eyes and a small smile appeared, a
   brightening smile in its meekness,
My heart was lost that day and I never lost that feeling from
   that day.

We did not speak, her gaze left mine, mine returned to
   the lake,
I knew that I must leave my time was spent.
As I stood next to this stranger lost in deepest thought,
   lost in grief,
I walked back from the dock, headed for my trail, headed for
   my space.

I had never felt this twinge that played on my heart,
I hoped that it would continue.
As I turned and looked back, towards this new emotion.
I knew that this was not the time, nor was this the place.

MISS YOU

You gave me life and I never cherished it when I was young,
You tried to show me good and I never took your heed.
You bathed me with love and I sometimes did not hear you,
You tried to be next to me always and I sometimes didn't
  realize your need.

You loved me with no return requested and I failed to return
  enough,
You tried to make me grow up and I failed to listen to you.
You pushed me to be better and I turned away at all the wrong
  times,
You tried to allow me to find my way and I turned not
  following you.

Now in the end, when there is no more time, I have lost all
  those things,
I can never get them back, you gave to me all of you.
I did not understand, I did not know, I would miss you,
I did not understand, I did not know, I would miss you so.

John G. Henning

MOON ENCOUNTER

I have been here before,
You have been here before,
We have gazed at each other under this same moon before,
Yet it is so new tonight.

I have seen this moon full of light,
You have seen this moon full of light,
We have hugged with all our strength beneath this moon full
  of light,
Yet it is so new tonight.

I have seen this moonbeam across the lake,
You have seen this moonbeam across the lake,
We have kissed with great passion with this moonbeam across
  the lake,
Yet it is so new tonight.

We have gazed at each other,
We have hugged with all our strength,
We have kissed with great passion,
Yet it is so new tonight.

MOON SHINE

Sometimes the moon is not full, but it still shines,
It shines on the lake that we face together.
It is our lake and our moon, when we are there,
It is ours to keep with the memories we share together.

Memories of a gentle touch, a caress, a loving hug,
Memories of a gentle peck, a warm touch of lips,
  a passionate kiss.
Memories of hearts beating, hearts resounding,
  hearts thumping together as one,
Memories of souls coming together, souls intertwined, souls
  wrapped one with the universe.

We can stand here for hours, in this place, which is our own,
For we know who we are, how we feel, what we really want.
To be together forever, to travel life hand in hand, to be with
  out fear,
Knowing that this is the life we want.

Life with each other's touch everyday,
Life with each other's kiss everyday,
Life with each other's heart everyday,
Life with each other's soul everyday.

This is our moon, this is our lake,
This is the time in ours lives that we can cherish forever.
Because it is our time, it is that time placed here for us,
And the love created will last forever.

John G. Henning

A love that electrifies with each touch,
A love that explodes with each kiss,
A love that embraces the heart,
A love that embellishes the soul.

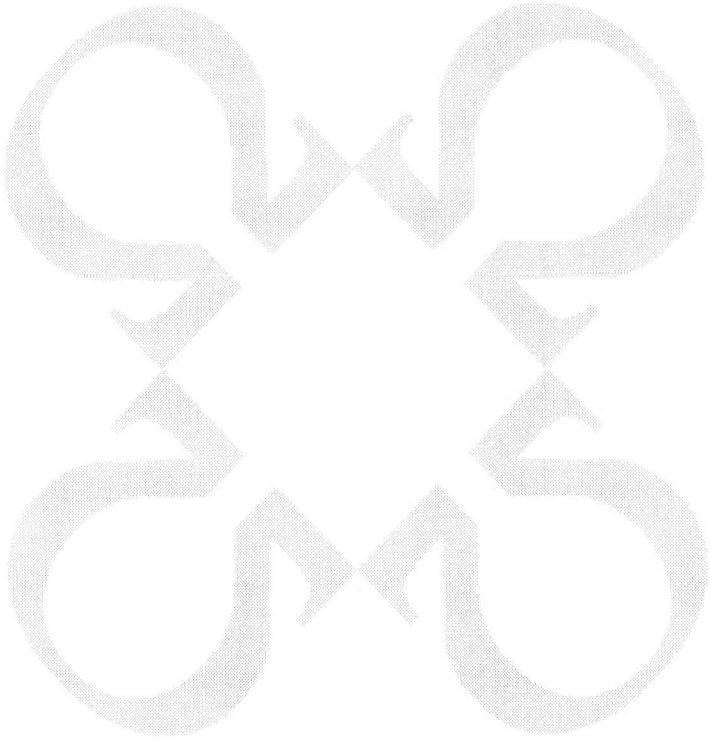

MOUNTAIN TREK

I guess it was the mystic thought of climbing a mountain,
Or the thought of just being above it all.
That set me on my goal of conquest seeking nothing but
　　that goal,
Seeing only that mountain that looks so small.

For I travel across the endless terrain so flat without elevation,
That my eyes gaze upon that peak.
So far away, yet so close that I cannot realize its height,
For this is that thing that I seek.

Ever closer the height changes into a majestic tower,
Reaching out for heaven, it is that need that calls.
That my neck would strain in search of the top,
And the walk is like scaling a fortress walls.

I am sure that many have traveled here as the path
　　leads upward,
But I feel I am the first, or at least the best.
I have never thought to even guess all the steps required,
To place me upon that enticing crest.

As nearer the sky comes, the harder the rise, the lifting of
　　my foot,
I will make it, I will be there.
And all of the world will dissolve in clouds,
For this is the height of my everywhere.

　　　　　　　John G. Henning

It is clear at the top and I can look towards the west,
This is not the top of the world.
For the mountain slides away out into the distance,
This is not the top of my world.

The mountain's feet abound out into endless lands,
This is but one mountain trek.
For beyond the vast plains, the ebbs of solitary silence,
This is but one life trek.

MUSHROOM

The dark, dank, dreary, dungeon is one of my homes,
Where the shining, shimmering, solar sun will never shine.
I thrive in the damp, dewdrop, drizzle, born by spores,
Living in the unseen, unknown, unused, universe of my mind.

Served whole, halved, hacked, homogenized for the mass,
I am the food, flavor, favorite, fundamental sustenance,
  of many.
Although cherished, chastised, cheapened, and championed for
  all causes,
But I am not a home, house, habitat nor hiding place of any.

John G. Henning

NEW GROWTH

The change has been so slight; it has been for quite sometime,
it is a good change,
Something has made this change in you, you are more
alive inside.
I can see it in the way you walk, the way you talk,
the way you smile,
It has been such a wonderful thing to see, this growth
from inside.

It brings a hint of fear, as there is so much to gain and so
much to lose,
The gains out weight the loss, but that loss will hurt so deep.
But the hurt will not change the feelings felt or created,
It will push them to the side and be buried deep.

There is more to this new growth then I could have imagined,
And yet this growth may have been caused by me, by my
own hand.
When this growth has been completed, when it has reached
its goal,
Then as much as I grabbed and held on, I will let go of
that hand.
My heart will always be with you, you will always live in
my soul,
I will stand on the side proud and true of this new growth.
And you will go on, and you will remember some of the time,
Mostly the thing you will remember is the new growth.

ONE HEART

A tiny little spark flashed across between us,
We did not know, we did not want to know it was there.
We talked in outer circles, we walked in silence,
For all that time we pushed aside all that was there.

As minutes became hours and hours became days,
It all came together, it rested in your heart and it rested in
  my heart,
There was always denial, this not real, it is but a fantasy,
Then one day we awoke new and refreshed, with one heart.

It is one heart that beats between you and I,
Not separate vessels inside separate shells.
Real and alive, beating slow and beating fast,
It knows no boundaries as it grows and swells.

This wonderful thing that grew from a spark,
It has learned to live in this new light; it has learned it
  belongs there.
We communicate beyond the circles and there is no silence,
Only when we wish to be silent, only when we are both
  together there.

As days become weeks and weeks become months,
This beautiful feeling, this luxurious feeling fills up each heart.
The fantasy has become reality, at least for a while, at least for
  the moment,
There is no separation of this feeling, we are one heart.

John G. Henning

It is one heart that beats between you and I,
Something we cannot change in all of our life.
It is one heart never to stop loving that, which it loves,
For we cannot change that which is our life.

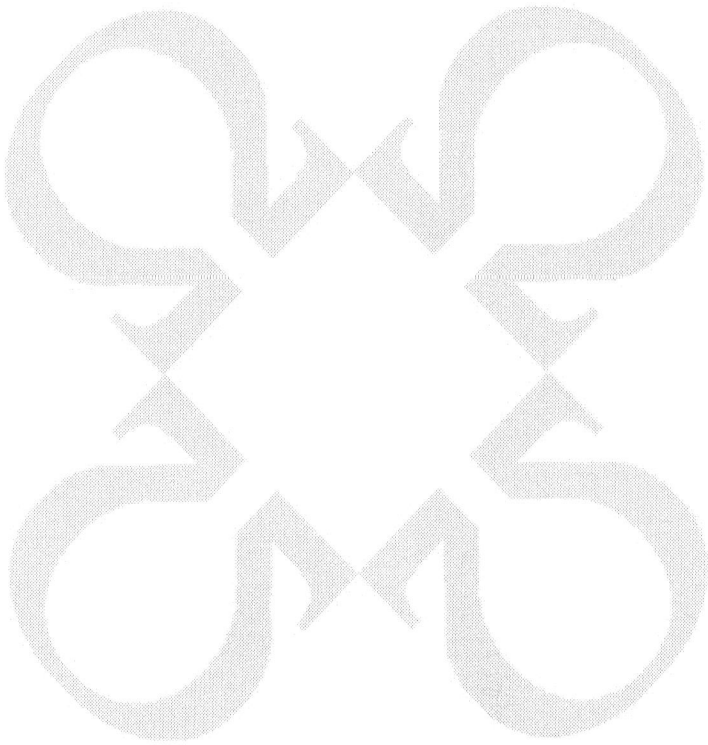

PASSION

A tiny dewdrop starts to flow gently etching its way along a
   plant stem,
Trudging onward heading for the point of shear drop, then
   melting into the soft earth.
The brook meanders along a silt bed, caressing the shoreline
   and tumbling over pebbles,
Embracing plant life, being kissed by sun, flowing out into the
   soft earth.

The stream born by unseen forces slithers through the
   foundation of stone,
Molding paths to be traveled for endless time, sliding off into
   the soft earth.
The river with pent-up rage, cuts through the rock of time,
   slamming into jagged edges,
Reaching gentle climax in a vast quiet bed, being spent into the
   soft earth.

The tiny spark fires up the heart asking it to follow the
   gentle path,
Dodging obstacles, caressing feelings, tumbling into an
   uncontrollable spin.
Being pressed to the limit by those things unseen, yet the
   foundation,
Peeking at the right time, most of the time, even without time,
   unable to win.

John G. Henning

The melting of a dewdrop, the embrace of life, the tumbling of emotions, molded paths, caressing feelings, unseen things, gentle climax of love,
The softness, which is passion.

PASSION PATH

The days have been filled with wondrous feelings,
here at our place,
Although it wasn't always ours, it has become that place for
us to go.
Out here with nature, spending countless hours in talk, in kiss,
in embrace,
Finding out all the things about each other, that we need
to know.

She has won my heart and I have captured hers, we are in love,
But until today, we have only been that shadow partner of
that emotion.
When does the time come, when is there a decision to change
this path,
To bind this love forever, to break down the barrier, to open
and extend the emotion.

Of all the smells I love in this forest, she brings the sweetest of
them all,
I am lost in her gazing eyes, trapped in the essence of her hair.
I am mesmerized by her voice, speaking always with her heart,
Tempted by kisses, engulfed in embrace, surrounded by our
place, there.

John G. Henning

Her skin is so soft and supple; I fear I am not worthy of
  that touch,
All of my emotion, all of my love, is here now, is here only
  for her.
All of the sights disappear, but all of the smells and the
  feelings remain,
I am lost forever in this passion of love, I am lost forever
  in her.

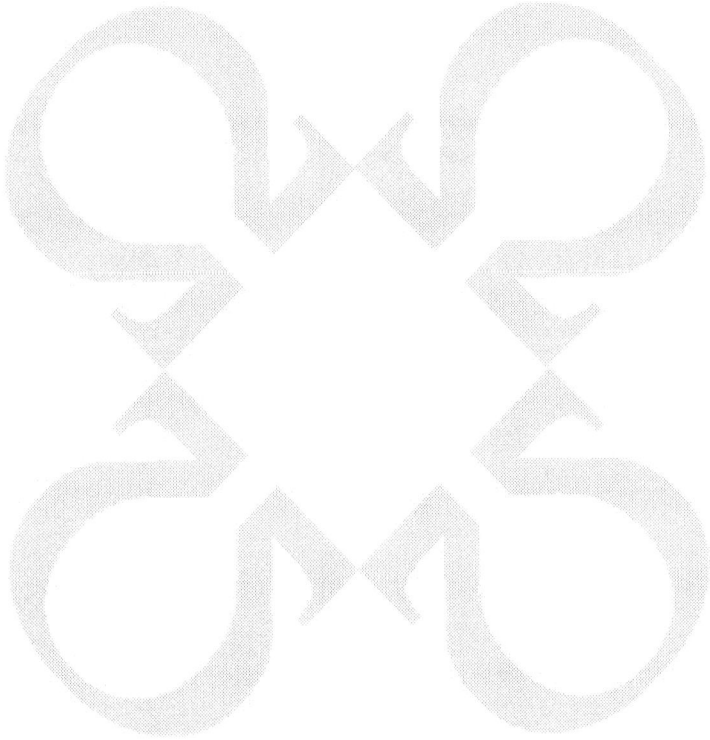

PASTEL LAKE

When the sun shines on the lake, the colors flow endlessly,
These delicate pastel colors, race across the still blue water.
Reflections of emotions whispered from loving lips,
Echo in the ripples of the smooth water.

Each color streaks in uneven lines from shore to shore,
Splashing color into eyes moist with pain, moist with love.
Pretty colors separate and yet still tied together,
Entwined like the strings of the heart lost in love.

When the sun sets it takes with it all of the colors,
The joys of color that sparkled in the eyes dies in darkness.
All those feelings trapped within the spectrum of light,
Fades in the unyielding coming of the endless darkness.

John G. Henning

PEACE

When you feel that it is wrong to travel this path,
You have created in need of life.
I wish you peace along the way,
For I hope that this is what you want in your life.

When reality hits like a stonewall, with no place to go,
And no one understands the feelings inside.
I bring you peace along the way,
For I know of those feelings locked up inside.

When life hands you a choice, a place to place your heart,
To be put in the hands of another.
I am that peace along the way,
For I am the one who understands, for I am the other.

PLUTO

This use to be a place were it was cold and dark,
Nowhere in this land was there the slightest hint of warmth
   or feeling.
It lay wasted, besieged by unwanting, battered by uncaring,
   left to isolation,
Never to see true light, never to hear laughter,
   never to have a feeling.

It existed only because it was there, a refuge for lost souls, a
   land with no love,
Those who tried to stay there without any feelings, perished
   without a trace.
Those who took away the souls of loves, buried their loves
   feelings deep in despair,
Never to see true love, never to feel, to live in the dark, buried
   without a trace.

A dawn has awakened in this land of dark, a resurrection of
   love, a true feeling,
Like a seed placed in the ground, it beckons for life,
   for existence, for love.
It is the true love, felt even in the dark catacombs of hearts
   eclipsed in gloom,
It is joyous, it is wonderful, it is all those things that make
   up love.

John G. Henning

Every look is a look that transports thoughts into reality,
Every word transcends all hearing, the words are real,
  the words are truth.
Every touch transforms emotion into a height of ecstasy,
Every kiss becomes the beacon of light into the heart,
  beaming with the truth.

This land is not a cold dark place where feelings are crushed,
This land is not a barren place, stripped of all love.
This land is the place of a rebirth, a trust in all those
  lost feelings,
This land is beautiful, this land is full of joy, this is a land now
  filled with love.

We walk this land with some inner fear, which melts within
  an embrace,
We walk this land with apprehension, which disappears in the
  look of love.
We walk this land with deep resolve, which dissolves in
  a gentle kiss,
We walk this land for we must; this is the land of love

PLUTO REPRISE

We walk along unknown trails created by our own desires,
We feel all those things we thought may have gone away from
  our hearts.
There has been so much fear, that we would lose those things
  we once had,
But reality has taken a different turn; it has shown us images of
  our hearts.

Those images are the warmth that can be felt, when there is
  warmth in return,
Those images are needs that that can be felt, when there is
  need in return.
Those images are words of truth flowing out like endless stars
  in a night sky,
Those images are feelings and emotions exploding to life like
  novas in a night sky.

We talk about those days when we felt and when feelings
  were returned,
We visualize days gone by, when times were good and fresh
  within our minds.
Our gaze goes out into that vast emptiness, knowing there is
  no answer,
Returning to those eyes of love, still fearing that hurt pictured
  within our minds.

John G. Henning

Those pictures were only of that one, the only one who could
ever be there, only that one,
Those pictures of fleeting joy, passing by slowly, leaving with
that one.
Those pictures we swore would never change, they would live
on forever,
Those pictures whose images of love, faded in time, seemingly
lost forever.

We feel those things born new in us; we are given
another chance,
The chance to feel alive again, to look and to see our very soul.
A whole new world, thought gone forever, unfolding before us
without hesitation,
Opening up all the closed emotions, bringing renewed feelings
to our soul.

Those feelings, which make our hearts, melt until they are one,
Those feelings, which make unwanted thoughts, disappear and
numb our minds.
Those feelings that make us see that we are but one
wondrous soul,
Those feelings that make us want to stay forever, to never
leave, to want to stay in love.

PORES

Every time you are near, every time I think of you,
I feel so alive, my mind becomes numb, I am enslaved to you.
My heart begins to pump madly; I cannot stop the feelings,
Traveling through all of my body, running through my veins,
   running out of my pores.

I become heated, I become sweaty, my mouth is dry,
Everything around me disappears; the world hides
   behind a cloud.
My muscles tense, my soul cries out, a void opens trying to
   drag me away,
Everything melts away; every emotion drains away, all of my
   inhibitions run out of my pores.

John G. Henning

RAIN

There has always been a mystical air about the rain, as I saw it,
Sometimes I saw it cause damage to plants and lives,
And yet it is the essence of those things that it could harm.

I have always liked the rain, to watch it fall from the first drop,
To watch it coat all that it touches in a watery hue,
To stand in its awe, to be mesmerized by its charm.

And the most important part of this fixation with rain,
Has been the time I spent with you under its umbrella,
Sheltered by a tree, nestled in your arms, lost in your embrace.

Drop by drop, some many at a time, some only one,
Dripping off of the trees, limbs, twigs and leaves,
Making its trek from the sky, to land upon your face.

To slowly move along your sculptured cheek, never in a
    straight line,
Seeking that next place to drop from, to continue the journey,
Finding the corner of kiss locked lips, becoming a part of
    them now.

Interlacing with the lined lips, unaware of its own existence,
Now lost in an existence, unaware that it is there, that it had
    come there,
Trickling past those lines as those lips part, reopened now.

Those single drops falling on hair, falling on clothes,
 dampening everything,
Everything but the embrace, the love, riveted against the rain,
 in love with the rain,
Hands touching wet cloth, lips touching wet skin, bodies
 through moisture being felt.

This love affair with the rain, with your soul, with your heart,
Never can be replaced, it resides whenever there is the rain,
It stands as you do against all odds, for we know we will
 not melt.

We will not melt from the rain; we will not be washed away by
 this rain,
Our love endures all those things that rain down on us,
We are strong and the only thing that will melt is our hearts.

So the rain stops but the love does not, it cannot, it does not
 know how,
We shiver from the rain and we quiver from the feelings
 and love,
The rain cannot take that away, cannot wash it away from
 our hearts.

John G. Henning

RISING MOON

We lean against the railing of the dock, this wooden terrace
  above the lake,
The breeze cools the sweat of heated brow, from being close,
  from being one.
The water is dark, there is no light, this looking glass view of
  the lake,
We await the appearance of the moon, the one and only one.

The rising moon reflects the feelings; we have shared as our
  love has risen,
From that small need buried deep in our hearts, waiting for the
  right moment.
Like the moon, the respect we have for all those things around
  us has risen,
We are here in the glow of the rising moon, here for this
  given moment.

Across the lake the moonlight follows us as we walk, hand in
  hand, heart in heart,
We know no boundaries, as we walk, no limits to the feelings
  crossing this gentle space.
Our feelings are strong and surge like emotional waves beating
  in each heart,
There are no other universes, there are no other worlds, there
  is just our own world, our own space.

The sweet smelling trees fills our lungs, we are trapped in the
web of spiders, in the web of love,
When we stop, we stop as one, touching lips, touching hearts,
and touching souls.
There is no explanation, there is no answer here, there is only
the feeling of true love,
That no matter what may happen, no matter who may come to
call, we are mates of our souls.

As the moon rises it no longer streaks across the water, it is
high in the sky, a spotlight of feelings,
It is focused, it is concentrated in just a small area, it reflects
back to where it came from this light.
The night becomes crisp, but we are warm, we will not deny
our feelings,
The silence echoes across the water, our reflections real, we are
bathed in this true light.

As we walk away from the lake, from the dock, from the moon
fully risen, we reflect on our lives,
Reflect back to the times when we shared these moments,
trapped in a memory forever.
We will always be able to remember these moments, always,
because they are our lives,
Even as times passes and life becomes trying, we will always
have the rising moon forever.

John G. Henning

SCARED

Scared, yes, I am scared, scared of these new feelings,
Scared, yes, I am scared, scared what these feelings can bring,
Scared, yes, I am scared, scared of what is wrong or right,
Scared, yes, I am scared, scared of why my heart sings.

Scared, yes, you are scared, scared of these new feelings.
Scared, yes, you are scared, scared what these feelings can bring,
Scared, yes, you are scared, scared of what is wrong or right,
Scared, yes, you are scared, scared of why your heart sings.

If we were not scared, these feelings would not be true,
If we were not scared, these feelings would be like so
   many others,
We are scared because we know that these feelings are true,
We are scared because we know these feelings are not like
   any others.

If we were not scared we would not know wrong from right,
If we were not scared we would lose those thoughts that hold
   us together,
We are scared because we know wrong from right,
We are scared because we know that we must be together.

As we travel through these feelings, feelings that explode inside,
As we travel through the right and wrong, destined to question
   it all,
We will be scared as the journey continues along this path of life,
We will be scared; we will be scared of it all.

SEARCHING FOR HEAVEN

I have been walking around in a daze, searching for heaven,
Searching high and low, in the light, in the dark, searching
 everywhere.
Where is heaven, what is heaven?
I thing that I use to know, when I was younger, when I
 was in love.

Now these days of searching has placed doubts in my mind,
Was I ever in love, did I really find heaven.
There were times when it seemed that heaven was right in
 front of me,
When I was sure of myself, when I felt I was in love.

Today I feel so different; I feel that maybe I have failed,
Maybe I am not being true to myself, not being true to you.
Leaving truth for reality, trying to leave feelings,
 breaking hearts,
When I know that there has never been a greater love.

Is my search over, this search for heaven, yes?
For heaven is in your eyes, it is in the touch of your fingertips.
Heaven is in the gentle kiss on my brow, an embrace held
 tightly,
Yes, heaven is here, it is in the warmth of your love.

John G. Henning

SEASONS

Spring is the season when love first blooms,
Everything is alive, all the feelings, all of the joy,
We seek those things that make us happy,
We venture into unknown areas of our lives.

Summer is the season when feelings warm up,
All that we touch makes passion rise,
We feel each other's inner self,
We want and need to share each other's lives.

Fall is the season when the heat of love cools,
The love is still there nestled in memories,
We need to share some open space,
We need to share other things in our lives.

Winter is the season when feelings go numb,
Numb from comfort, those feelings still exist in other ways,
We want each other's company for the rest of life,
We want our feelings to again be a part of our lives.

Seasons are not everywhere and people do not share them all,
Our springs can last forever, if we listen to each other,
Our summers can remain warm, if we talk with each other,
Our falls can be warmed by the memories of spring,
Our winters do not have to exist with summer feelings in
    our lives.

All of the seasons are there inside of us,
We use those that we want, if we wish,
If we remember what those seasons are,
If we remember how they feel,
They will last and they will be a part of us, all of our lives.

John G. Henning

SECOND CHANCE

One day the world ended, in shattering tears that etched
  a heart,
For the true love of life left on the wind of pain,
That day when professed love no longer mattered,
  it had been buried,
Buried inside a heart that could never be the same.

A small piece came back and the joy returned, there were
  great moments,
Full of finding out new horizons, venturing into unknown
  places,
Pleasant memories filled with new love for all that it was
  worth,
Beautiful days, loving thoughts, wondrous beaming faces.

As the days wane, reality hits the nerve of lost love,
The seed of hurt that lay dormant, starts to grow again,
There is never a real cause, it happens for no reason,
At least none that is apparent, nothing that can be given
  a name.

But there is always that second chance, that time of real love,
When it stands up and pulls at your heart, and will not let go,
It has smoothed that heart, taken away the pain, turned life
  around,
It has brought back love, as a second chance for this is all we
  know.

SECOND GUESS

It has never really mattered that we are not alike in all ways,
It has mattered that we cared enough for each other to accept
  those ways.
The path we have walked has created barriers, sometimes with
  no doorway out,
But walking the path together has provided a break in the
  barrier, creating a doorway out.

We do not second guess the things that we do, for we do things
  with considered feelings,
We do not second guess the logic, for we are aware of each
  other's feelings.
Living each day with the future as a big open space of
  opportunity, a chance to explore,
Provides a new future so vast and large, opening pathways to
  feelings which we can explore.

We may not be the same in every way, and the paths may have
  many barriers without a door,
But we should never second guess the feelings we have, or the
  future we can explore.

John G. Henning

SECRETS

The water glistens as it babbles, blindly over boulders turned
  to smooth stone,
Through crystal clear vision lies sand and tan and brown stone.

Gaze deeply into the brown stone of the earth for it holds the
  deepest of secrets,
But there are deeper realms within life, deep within eyes that
  hold secrets.

SLINKY STEPS

It is said that we learn from all the things we see,
And that we name name's of things we do not know.
So if that's happen to you, don't let it get you down,
Because you are who you are and that is all you need to know.

So those legs have gotten you in trouble, their ostrich I believe,
But I only know that an ostrich takes long and determined
  steps.
So if you have that title, and surely it must have been in jest,
Because the reality is that those legs take long and slinky steps.

SMILE

It use to be that there never was a smile on this face,
Maybe because there was no happiness, maybe because there
  had been.
With life's changes comes realization that life can be grand,
And a smile emerges where the frown had been.

The smile is still not always there, because life has set
  up barriers,
And reality lifts its head up high, and says not today my friend.
But time wears away those obstacles for they never should
  have been there,
And the trusted smile becomes larger with a trusted friend.

So if I am to be given, this time that we call life,
Then let it be that everyday that at sometime I smile.
And if life can give me the time to wear away the barriers,
Then someday with life's help, I will wake up with a smile.

SMILING LADY

If I could be anything in the world, I would like to be your
  smile,
For it is the brightest thing on this earth and probably
  in heaven.
I feel so privileged to be the recipient of that smile,
That I try to smile as bright, knowing I could not reach that
  heaven.

Of course that could not happen, since that smile is a part of
  your heart,
So vast with love and affection for all those who seek its
  warmth.
My heart though not as large, tries so hard to be like you,
I am forever in your debt that I might receive just a portion of
  that warmth.

Your eyes are the beacons of that heart, sending out rays of love,
If I could just be the catcher of that force, I could live in love
  forever.
Anyone who has gazed into the glow of your love and
  happiness,
Could never in their wildest dreams, not love you, not love you
  forever.

If I could be anything in the world, I would like to be your
  smile,
For I would be in the midst of love, next to a forever glowing
  heart.

John G. Henning

And my heart would be filled with love and life and my eyes
  would be filled with happiness,
For I would never leave this place, for it would be my heart,
  too.

This ode is for you, my smiling lady, who weathers the
  toughest of storms,
I will always try to return that smile, when you may not be able
  to smile.
For I know that if I try really hard, believing with all my might,
I may make a sad day a little brighter with my own little smile.

STEEL SNAKE

Slithering through the valley, the steel pressed against wood
  aiming for the earth's heart,
Baked in glare when the sun is high and hot, glistening in the
  night as the moon travels along its curves.

A destination setup to provide a way to travel along the world's
  corridors,
To defy the laws of nature, to plunge into that world, to nestle
  on the ground that it serves.

The pinging travels for miles as the train, weighting against the
  steel, forces its sections to rise,
And the wheel slams into that rise, creating that echo which
  bounces off sheer rock.

While in the turns the steel cries out, bending under this force
  so great and unyielding.
Pounded and pounded with no mercy, a never-ending
  movement of a never-ending clock.

The snake crosses the river high above that water, protected by
  the towering structure,
And the creaking and the groaning play harmony with clanging
  of wheels against the steel.

For the train that travels along its back, does not know that
  which is under it,
And there is no feeling for both, for the snake is not real.

John G. Henning

SON

I know that I dart around like an untiring force,
Running without end, leaving mild destruction in my wake.
I have so much energy and of course it runs amuck,
I really don't have control; it is some force I cannot break.

So when you look at me and tell me things to do,
And I look back like I'm somewhere else, and I don't seem
  to care.
It's not that I don't understand, it's just something I must live
  with and try to control,
But that won't happen for years and that might not seem fair.

I am not like my sister or you with the control of saints,
I must be doing something all the time, even though nothing
  gets done.
But there is something that I will always have energy for,
Something that forces will never change, I will always be
  your son.

SPECIAL SPOT

Sometimes it is a place,
Sometimes it is in our hearts.

We all have that special spot, maybe from childhood, maybe
   from today,
It is a spot very dear to us, in sight, in sound and smell.
We know it in an instant, it belongs to us forever,
   this growing need,
Something we cannot stop rising inside, something we
   cannot quell.

It is this special spot; we all look for in earnest and in
   loving care,
Even if we are unaware that we do, that we search for
   this place.
For we know that when we find this paradise, this Shangri-La,
   this utopia,
We will remember it forever, frozen in space and time.

We may return here to this place we call our own,
Return knowing in our heart that it will remain the same.
Only because we live that moment of first recognition,
We live the day, we live the second and it is never the same.

We bring to our spot those who we love, sometimes it is not
   our mother or father,
We bring to this spot those who we love, sometimes it is not
   child or partner or even those who are our friends.

John G. Henning

We bring to our spot those who we love with our total heart,
  whoever they might be,
We bring to our spot those who will forever be one with us
  more than our true friends.

So with this special spot, we bring forth all those dreams that
  are ours,
We bring forth all those hopes deep in our soul.
We bring forth all those ideals we hope to share,
We bring forth our belief that one day we bring the one who
  will be our soul.

And when that day comes, we will treasure it forever,
Whether it is a place or a place in our heart.
For we will know that which we share,
Is so much more than a place, it is our heart.

This special spot will be ours forever,
For we own that portion of time.
We know that no matter what life brings,
This special spot is our life for all time.

SWEET HAPPINESS

The gleam in your eye, the radiance of your smile, the glow of
   your face,
They have kept me here, near your heart; close enough to meld
   as one,
And you have made that possible being here, being yourself,
For this is the only place I want to be, the only place in my life.

You are always yourself with me; you are always that
   kind person,
The one that stole my heart and ran away with it as their own,
Although there have been times, when things did not seem to
   work out,
Too many complications, too many thoughts, too many paths
   in life.

The paths have been easier to walk with, with you, with your
   guiding light,
A light that is a beacon that shines in the night, putting fears
   to sleep,
Fears found out not to be real, just imagined in the mind,
   created out of unknowing,
Unknowing that there is a sweet happiness in life.

John G. Henning

That sweet happiness of life has been mine for a time, even if
  too short,
And my heart has been given so much sweetness, that it could
  never hold it all,
I treasure those times and times to come, I hope that I am able
to return that sweetness,
For you are to me that sweet happiness of life.

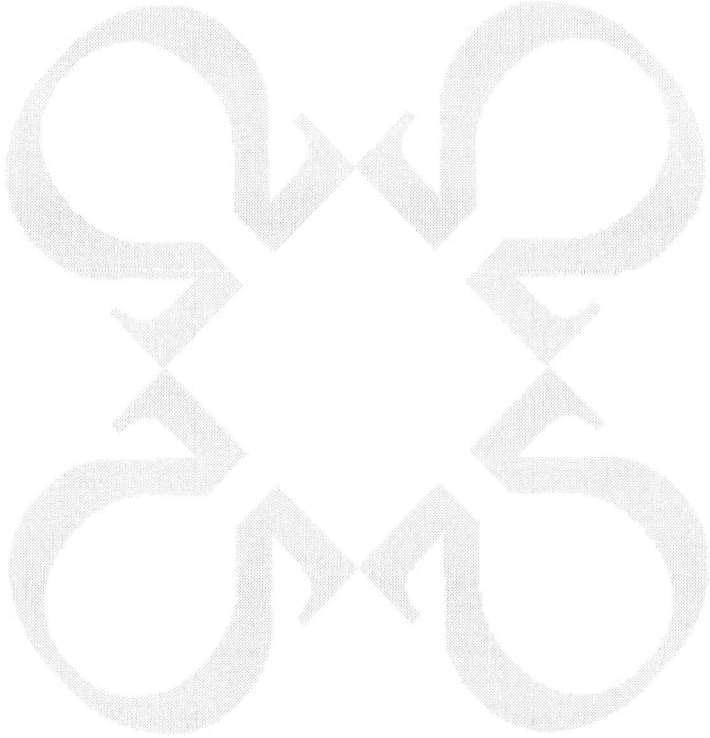

TEMPTATION TRAIL

Summer days can be very long or very short, depending on
  our feelings,
This one has been long and my trek along the trail a long one.
But I was soon to come to my special place, just a smooth flat
  boulder facing the lake,
A large as the dock across the lake, so smooth, cooled by tree
  shadows and baked by the sun.

I sat here for endless hours, without worry, without cares,
All of the times that I had come to this lake, to my summer
  retreat.
This time it was different somehow, I carried a new emotion,
A love, a feeling, something unknown by me, something I did
  not seek.

She came out of the shadows of the trail; walking opposite I
  would think,
At least different from my own walking patterns, and I
  was startled.
I knew in an instant who she was, her mousy brown hair
  captured in the sunlight,
She stepped back realizing my presence, also a bit startled.

I smiled and she returned a smile that lit up the shadows,
Only though the eyes of love, of course, only in my mind's eye.
She came to sit next to me, this flat sanctuary, now shared,
And the swell of my heart was as big as the open sky.

John G. Henning

She told my about her reasons for being there, some very
  saddening thoughts,
But that now somehow the lake, the trees, the air, had set
  her free.
At least for the moment at hand, at least for today, at least
  for yesterday,
No one could know how long that feeling might be.

We sat there for hours talking and joking feeling so at ease,
Never really locked in eye contact, still avoiding that
  temptation to stare.
As the day wore on and the time had come to leave,
There came a time when eye contact came, and would always
  stay there.

It was a long silent walk back, passed the house where she
  was staying,
A quick good-bye, no contact, not that special look, just a
  quick glance.
But it was a glance that sent the waves of emotion crashing in
  my chest,
I hoped to one day take charge of that feeling, if I should get
  the chance.

THE BENCH

When we sit that way, the way that lovers sit, nestled in each
   others arms,
I know that I feel for you with all of my heart and I am aglow
   with this feeling.
I hope in my heart, in my soul and my mind, that you feel
   the same,
You are so warm and tender, you are so real, you are
   the feeling.

We scan this lake before us, mesmerized by the feelings inside,
Warmed by those feelings so much, we must surely glow in
   the darkness.
I feel you so deeply, I cannot feel anything else, I am numb,
As we gaze into the reflection on the lake, we gaze into
   the darkness.

We both see the hope that there is, even if it is in this fantasy,
But it is also a dream, a dream shared by both of our hearts.
It cannot be denied, but you will do this deed, you will deny it,
And all those things that you wish will be trapped in
   our hearts.

We will always treasure these feelings, they are real, they are
   not fantasy,
The little seed of doubt buried in your heart will not allow
   it to grow.
I will be here for sometime, I want to be here forever, with you,
When you have decided, I will be here and we can grow.

John G. Henning

THE DANCE

We have been together for quite some time now,
We have shared many hours of deep discussions,
We have shared many hours of gazing silence,
But we have never been to the dance.

We have know each other for quite some time now,
We have shared troubled times when all seemed lost,
We have shared laughs about ourselves as we found ourselves,
But we have never been to the dance.

We have cared for each other for quite some time now,
We have shared treasured moments locked in memories
We have shared open feelings trapped inside for so long,
But we have never been to the dance.

We have loved each other for quite some time now,
We have shared all that is in our hearts and veins,
We have shared all those feelings that make up the world,
Don't fear now, don't turn away, it is just a dance.

THE LIVING ROSE

The new fresh dew plays against the soft petal of the rose,
Streaming down like a tear of joy, with smiles abound,
Headed towards the unknown, meandering along the way,
Hanging for an instant before crashing to the ground.

Basking in the stream of light, drying out the tears,
Swelling up with the heat of life, bursting towards that source,
Losing the life force fluid in the process, searching deeply
    for replacement,
Trapped in the cycle of life, trapped in the life force.

Without the fluid, without the heat, without the light,
The petal becomes so rough and brittle, ebbing out the life,
The luster fails, the shine dulls, the texture of lifeless prevails,
The rose is a rose no more and life is not life.

John G. Henning

THE MISSING SONG

If we never missed floating clouds across blue skies,
If we never missed the sunny skies and dew upon flowers,
If we never missed the laughter of a child,
Then we have missed life.

If we never missed the tranquil waters of a lake in summer,
If we never missed snow covered grass reaching out for
   the sun,
If we never missed the friendship of a single friend,
Then we have missed life.

If we never missed those who made us and nurtured us
   through life,
If we never missed trials and tribulations beckoning
   for resolve,
If we never missed someone we loved when we had gone away,
Then we have missed life.

If we never missed love turned away and etched with pain,
If we never missed joy and laughter when it could return,
If we never missed true love's touch each and everyday,
Then we have missed life.

THE PARK

I did not know where you were taking me that day,
That day when I knew for sure I never wanted to leave
  your side.
You took me to the park, not large, not small, just right,
Right for us, right for the feelings we both felt inside.

I loved being with you in the park, to walk along paths
  through grass,
And along the lake that nestles against the rocky knoll.
To sit and talk and watch the world go by, oblivious to its
  passing,
Not caring at this moment, that life and its burden may take
  its toll.

I wanted to tell you that day; I wanted to profess my love,
But I was afraid that you might run away forever.
I looked in your eyes and could see that maybe I was right for
  that day,
That you might not want it to last forever.

But you put your head against my shoulder, and I placed my
  arm around you,
I could feel the warmth of your body, the warmth that you
  have inside.
I wished that I could harness that warmth, to be the keeper of
  that warmth,
I would make it shine from you, never letting it run away
  and hide,

John G. Henning

And I would take that warmth and combine it with the warmth
  I felt,
Sending it out for all to see, not caring about their thoughts,
  caring about us.
There came a time then, that I though that I was right, that it
  could not last forever,
I did not proclaim the right to your warmth, the right to us.

The touches, the embraces, those warm feelings only allowed
  to be felt by some,
I felt them with you and you with me in this pristine place,
  our place.
Nothing in the world can change those moments or these
  new memories,
Memories that will reside in our minds, our hearts and our
  souls, in our place.

I have never in my life felt the way that I did that day,
It was as if my cold heart had opened up ready for love.
But just as it did, it shutdown, just like yours,
  cluttered in thought,
And neither of us could say it, make the bond of love.

Those sweet things said, those troubled feelings stay here,
They are a part of us, yet still a part of this park, our park.
The loving touches, the tender kisses, the deep hugs melted
  as one,
They remain here forever, a memory of this place, this park.

THE SPOT

It is very nice this spot, this spot that we enjoy,
This spot that shows us the sun rising and setting, and the
  moon in all its stages,
This spot, is a very nice spot.

It is very nice this spot, this spot where we stand,
Holding on to each other, holding on to a dream, holding on to
  this fantasy,
This spot is a wonderful spot.

This is very nice this spot, this spot where we kiss,
Ever so lightly, ever so tenderly, ever so deeply,
This spot is a fabulous spot.

It is very nice this spot, this spot that feels our warmth,
This warmth born on love, caressed in caring, generated by
  these feelings,
This spot is a warm spot.

It is very nice this spot.
This spot that we enjoy,
This spot where we stand,
This spot where we kiss,
This spot that feels our warmth,
This spot is our loving spot.

John G. Henning

THE WALK

I am in the dark as to where I am going,
I know that I want to go more than anything in the world.
There is still the fear of what may happen,
Is it all right? Can I live in this new world?

If I decided not to walk, would it change my life forever?
Can I give that which I want so much up so quickly?
I think not, I cannot, there is no reason to do that,
And as fast as doubt has risen, it is gone so quickly.

It is only gone because of you, I could not do this without you,
You are the focus, you are the impetus, you are the reason.
As long as there is breath in my body, as long as I can feel the
    way I do,
There is no doubt, there is the trust, there is the reason.

It may not have been that way all of the time, who knows
    when it really starts,
The look, the touch, the need, the desire, when did it become
    real.
I guess we never really know, we guess, we dodge, we make so
    many excuses,
The end result is that yes it has happened and yes it is real.

The walk has made me alive again; my inside has grown to like
　　this feeling,
I don't want it to end, I will never try to end it, I will not end it.
Yet I know that if there is no feeling, if it travels to someone
　　else,
I will want to end it, I will try to end it, I will end it.

The walk is not about the lovely trees, and shrubs and
　　beautiful houses,
It is about who we are, but what are we, where do we stand,
　　how do we walk.
We have decide on this trek together, we will face this trek
　　together,
Believing in what the dream can be or the fantasy, we can still
　　do the walk.

John G. Henning

THREE SCOOP

SCOOP ONE

It is the age of innocence, what is there that I like about you,
You are fresh and new, you smile from inside,
What makes you so special to me, I am lost, I'm a lost soul,
You question and probe, I do too, looking for the inside.

Smiling through glass etched with rain, you wave; I forgot who
    you are,
My mind is lost in other things, grief, sorry, complex thoughts,
There is too much work, my heart has broken,
    I do not know why,
You are alive, you are real, the soul mate of my thoughts.

You are so kind and sweet, yet you hurt so much, I see it in
    your eyes,
You have the same grief, a pain never realized before; I need to
    help you,
But can I do that, I can barely help myself, I must, I need to,
    I will,
And yet in this hour there is a lot to learn, I lot to know
    of you.

The pain in your eyes comes from so many other areas; I am at
   a loss to find them all,
Is this a quest started by you, by me, are we really that
   new feeling,
Your voice echoes in my mind, you crowd my heart I am in fear,
I do not know if you will ever feel this feeling.

But why do I pursue, why do you, are you looking for me,
What is the attraction, maybe there is none; we are in a dream,
The days travel on, more thoughts come to mind, I am for you,
Are you for me, why all of this masking of an enchanted dream.

Will I ever find the real you, will I show you the real me,
We embrace in the circle of friendship, but have we already
   crossed the line,
No, we are still with faculties, we still cherish the space ahead,
Yet we have already been there, we mimic the sands with lines.

John G. Henning

SCOOP TWO

You are so happy, I am so happy and yet I cry,
I am way beyond any thoughts that held me back, in check
  of myself,
We walk away each day with a piece of each other not
  knowing that we do that,
I am afraid to let you know I am afraid of myself.

Long gracious walks through time, learning more of each other,
That which you fear the most has come to rest in your heart,
You grieve in this time of mourning, I am helpless,
  I am not there,
I have failed you soul mate, I thought that there was another in
  your heart.

I did not know there was so much to learn, we share the
  feelings as they grow,
Embraces become real, empathy increases, there is a
  real feeling,
I feel this feeling, this real thing, do I dare ask the question,
I must, but can I, I can, I do and no is the answer to this
  feeling.

I am at a loss, I hurt in a one sided blitz, but there is more here,
A longing has arisen even in the attempt to keep that
  longing away,
In the rain, embraces have turned to kisses, delicate in
  their touch,
Even with all this new emotion, it still must be pushed away.

When does it happen, when does that feeling grab on and not
let go?
Was it hidden behind the painted face, that which accepts
reality,
Have we both known that this is the place we want to be?
This is the place where there is fantasy, with smaller pieces
of reality.

You are so innocent; I am so innocent, yet we are one in a quest,
We are there is this veil of friendship, we are beyond that
which can hold us back,
Time has made us one; we do not like that, yet we enjoy
each other,
We have learned some inner thoughts without saying a word,
we cannot go back.

John G. Henning

SCOOP THREE

This is not right, this is wrong; we cannot do this,
We try with all of our might, as individuals to fight this battle,
  this growing feeling,
Over and over again we learn about ourselves, we need to
  know many things,
Have we gone past the point of no return when physical has
  become the feeling?

I want you more that anything in my life; I cannot express
  it enough,
Yet life has put me through new grief, I do not know if I can
  make it through life,
My heart has broken; I have lost that love I thought real many
  bygone moments ago,
The test has come again, the test to go on when life is taken
  from life.

You are there in my need, you really are, I have let fear leave
  this place,
I try to prove that feeling has gone to love; I want you to know
  that, I want you to feel love,
But who am I to think that you are not with love, I am the fool
  to think this thought,
You are so right; to say there is emotion, and yet not total love.

But that is not how we feel, the emotions are too strong, they
  explode inside,
We are trapped in the web of loving, the struggle is to no avail,
  we cannot fight,
Yet as we get closer, we repel each other hoping that this will
  not go on,
And not wanting to leave unharmed, we leave without a fight.

Alas this best plan falls besides the road of life; it cannot
   be real,
The only real is the pounding of hearts drowning out any other
   sound of life,
Each kiss has created its own reality, each embrace its
   own world,
We cannot go back to that which was, we must continue on
   through life.

We have reached that point when all else has failed, we cannot
   leave each other,
We cannot give up each other, yet we cannot give up our lives,
They are real, the reality and the fantasy, we are so close we are
   really one,
We are intertwined with each other; we are intertwined in
   our lives.

And so we are at that point in life, where we decide what we
   are to do,
There are no easy solutions, yet one is not to ever give
   ourselves up for love,
For we would not do justice to ourselves or to anyone else for
   whom we care,
This is not about not loving; it is about too much of this
   emotion that is love.

John G. Henning

TOUCH ME

There are times when life is so strange and we come together
  for no reason,
At least no reason that we can think of or want to think of,
It is all wrong, we know that, but there is still that chance,
A chance that if I would let you, you would touch me.

It has been long and hard this road that bends,
  twists and turns,
If I stay in one place too long in my mind, you are gone,
Ventured out of my grasp, ventured out to some new place,
While all the time I thought, I was there for you to touch me.

Every precious second of time, like sand spilling away, causes
  too much pain,
Pain that sometimes even now, hurts so deep that there is
  little hope,
Hope that I can be in your grace again, hope I will not
  fear again,
Hope that you will touch me, again.

TREASURED MOMENTS

Sometimes I wonder how it could get any better,
Sometimes I wonder how I could feel this way, how can I feel
 this way.
I have been here before; at least I thought I was,
And then I find that I never really was there, not this way.

Each touch, each thought brings on treasured moments,
There is so much feeling and reality in that feeling.
There cannot be any denial, there is no turning around,
The joy is beyond all other things, it is the true feeling.

Finding out that this love is so good, yet knowing that it can be
 so bad,
For we know that with this love there can be a troubled soul.
Troubled because of the care for others, the understanding of
 their own feelings,
Yet we cannot deny all of the good, we cannot deny this
 loving soul.

So these treasured moments rush into our hearts, filling it up
 with warmth,
And in our doubt we realize there is no other place we can be
 go but with love.
For the feelings being felt, the emotions crashing inside, the
 tears shed,
Belong to us in these treasured moments, for all of this is
 our love.

John G. Henning

TRUE KISS

There are so many things that happen during the time when
  love blossoms,
So many moments of listening, of talking, of hugging,
  of embracing
Touching a hand, a face, a cheek, a forehead,
  exploring new avenues,
Trying to understand this new feeling, never felt before with
  such force.

You cannot let go; love won't let you, let go
You are bound to this trail, this journey into new
  understanding, new feelings,
There are so many places to go in your mind, in your soul, in
  your heart,
You are a slave to this new and exciting life; you are a slave to
  a new course.

You wait for the other to know, to realize all these new feelings,
You wait because you know that it is more real then life itself,
Along comes the true kiss, the one you both have waited for all
  of your life,
It makes your heart sweat, it makes your soul melt, it makes
  your mind block out the world.

You will never be the same again; you will never feel as great as
   you do today,
For there is no finer thing in this world then true love,
There is nothing finer than a true kiss,
Because all that you want, all that you need, arrived with this
   new world.

John G. Henning

TRUTH

Truth is but a small part of the overall picture of life,
Yet it is the glue that holds it together.

It comes in many forms and is never the same twice,
Because life grows and expands everyday.

Truth can be the whole essence of a relationship,
Or it can be its demise.

So truth is what we hold as truth, not words but thoughts
  and action,
One day we will learn to understand that, one day.

TURN AROUND

Sometimes we are right in front of you, but you do not see,
And we speak the language of love, but you return no sound.
Sometimes life makes it possible for us to sit alone,
But just for once be in our sights, turn around.

And if we cause you pain of which we have no knowledge,
We too suffer with open sorrow, which knows no mortal
  bound.
For we cherish your life, your love, your feelings,
We will always be here if needed, turn around.

And when the day comes that we are of no further service,
Do not fret, we have loved and we have been found.
But if you do not wish to take that love for free,
And maybe bring some renewed hope, then let us go away,
  turn around.

John G. Henning

TURTLE

It's not so much that you lumber along with minimum care in
  the world,
Or glide through seemingly familiar waters with an unknown
  grace.
It's not so much that your shell provides a false security to
  your world,
Or that you glide through life with elegant grace.

It's knowing that the day brings renewed light and peace for
  a time,
And you can believe in the feeling hidden deep inside.
It's knowing that today may not be the same, at least for a
  short time,
And you can focus and awaken that feeling deep inside.

It's about being alive in the world so immense with challenge,
Sometimes fearful of the results of the day.
It's about living up to and fighting for the right of challenge,
Sometimes fearful of the results at the end of the day.

For life has chosen to lead you along that which is so unknown,
And it's not so much the thought of being a turtle.
For life has chosen to provide the challenge with this new
  unknown,
And it's not so much the thought, as it is becoming that turtle.

WOODEN WALK

The air is alive with freshness, as a breeze blows through
  the leaves,
The walk is special it is shared with the one who enjoys the
  wooden walk.
The sun and sometimes the moon, shines through, lighting up
  two smiling faces,
It is a pleasure to share this walk, this wooden walk.

Although we know that there are creatures looking at us, as we
  look for them.
Sometimes with their life, they cross the path of the wooden
  walk.
Rain may come but is doesn't matter, we will not melt,
Not on the walk of walks, the wooden walk.

We cherish those times both old and new, relishing the feeling
  of life,
Stride for stride in this walk, the wooden walk.
The steps are too numerous to count and they will go on
  forever, if we wish,
The walk is today, or tomorrow, the wooden walk.

So we will continue to find those places where the woods
  engulf us
And enjoy every step of the walk, the wooden walk.
So if I might and I will always want to share,
Can I walk with you on the wooden walk?

John G. Henning

WALKING WITH ME

It was very hard to tell you that day, it was very hard to leave
  the next day,
All of the fears that had been suppressed were realized in an
  instant.
These days would never be forgotten, memories will make
  them last forever and a day,
Memories would also remember you walking with me.

Like a ghost we may fear, or one that we may love,
  your presence was always there,
It helped me through the sorrow; it helped me through
  the pain.
I knew that no matter where life would lead me now, you
  would always be there,
Traveling this part of the road of life, walking with me.

I know that you wanted to be there, to share the sorrow, to mix
  our tears,
I know that you wanted to hold me in your gentle arms and
  rock away the hurt.
In my loneliness, in my time of sorrow, those shed tears were
  our tears,
And I never felt that you were not walking with me.

We go on with life; we try to figure out why it hurts so badly
  some times,
Why must we be alone now, why must we miss that person
  we loved.
Our sorrow is replaced by thoughts of goodness, of new and
  better times,
You will always be there walking with me.

John G. Henning

WALKING THE LINE

As we travel through life sometimes the line of life is bold,
Many times there are too many forks, fractures of time.
If we believe in life and that life can brings us love,
Then there is only joy when walking the line.

Sometimes we stubble and the line becomes obscure and
  unclear,
If we are fortunate we meet someone with love's mind.
We still do not believe and we let that time pass,
And like the shaky tightrope we cannot walk the line.

Because we have become too convinced that it's not true,
Truth can only be found in the trying, not by some looking sign.
We pass just once through that cloud radiant with true love,
If we walk by this moment, we never again walk the line.

For the line disappears rubbed out like the line in the sand,
Blown away as just fabrication, can we be so blind.
Some of us can see that line of life and love; we do not
  pass it by,
Even if we are the only players, at least we walk the line.

WHISPER OF LOVE

Soft breezes caress the dandelion, spreading the seed of life,
Gently placing the seed where life can grow,
Whisper of love

The slow rhythmic breathing of the child, expelling treasured
  breaths,
Caught by the cheek of the mother, nestling the child,
Whisper of love.

Gently floating leaves, carried on soft waves of air,
Brushing the hair of the young woman,
Whisper of love.

A tender endearment captured in the realm of hearing,
Breathed so low and enchanting, voiced loud and clear inside,
Whisper of love.

Gentle mists laying silken drops on weathered cheeks,
Bathing the rough texture of the aging man,
Whisper of love.

A kiss of life brought about by only one,
Awaiting all who seek the truth about life's,
Whisper of love.

John G. Henning

YESTERDAY'S DREAMS

They swirl around in a vortex, like fallen leaves in fall, yester
  day's dreams,
Battered by emotions, spewed out in all directions, separated
  by fears.
These dreams held so dear by more than one, cherished as the
  life itself,
Broken down till there is nothing left but tears.

When they were alive, when they were a part of life, they were
  today's dreams,
Somehow, some way they changed, changed by an unknown
  force.
They left without warning, they left their mark,
  they left quickly,
Headed down the sea of life, headed to no end, off course.

Yesterday's dreams, who wants them, who cares for them,
But for a while they were all that existed, existed for the hour,
  for a day, for another day.
They were wanted, they belonged, they were more than real,
Now they are cast away, they recede in the memory; they do
  not live another day.

www.ingramcontent.com/pod-product-compliance
Lightning Source LLC
Chambersburg PA
CBHW031853090426

42741CB00005B/478